Making
Ribbon Leis 2
More Handmade Gifts of Aloha

Coryn Tanaka
and May Masaki

BESS
PRESS

3565 Harding Ave.
Honolulu, Hawai'i 96816
Phone: (808) 734-7159
Toll Free: (800) 910-2377
Fax: (808) 732-3627
www.besspress.com

Design: Carol Colbath

Photos on pages 3 (#5), 4, 5, 6, 7, 8, 9 (#1), 10, and 11 by Reginald Yee,
Ace Portrait Studio; on pages 3 (#3), 19 (#2), 23 (#1 and #2), 29 (lei), 34
(lei), 40 (#1-2), and 42 by Caryl Nishioka; all other photos by Carol Colbath

Library of Congress Cataloging-in-Publication Data

Tanaka, Coryn.
  Making ribbon leis 2: more
handmade gifts of aloha /
Coryn Tanaka and May Masaki.
      p. cm.
  Includes illustrations.
  ISBN 978-1-57306-170-4
  1. Leis - Hawaii. 2. Leis.
I. Masaki, May. II. Title.
SB449.5.L4.T36 2003 745.923-dc21

Printed in China

~ Contents ~

Acknowledgments

~ Special mahalos to ~

Our extended family at Flora-Dec Sales: Sidney Hamada, LiSa Kaneshiro, Mac, Ken, Verge, Cory, Leanne, and Wanda, for without their help this book wouldn't have been possible; our Mōʻiliʻili Community Center staff, Barbara, Leimoni, and Jill; Cleo Kanai, owner and operator of Creations by Cleo on Kauaʻi, as well as her students. And our best friends Ben and Muriel Yin, who are like parents to me, and to their family Wendy, Melanie, Hoku, and Ikaika, who helped with our first book. Our family from the Bess Press, the staff at Booklines, and Wendy Arbeit for putting up with Mom and me during so many hours of hard work.

Our fabulous students at Mōʻiliʻili Community Center: Kathrine, Edith, Lily, Carolyn, Kimie, Naomi, Miyoko, Shizuko, Shizue, Lucy, Ruby, Caryl, Sandy, and Hazel; and our terrific students at Kānewai District Park: Diane, Sherry, Gail, Judi, Kali, Colleen, Amy, Cynthia—with our first book they became famous overnight. And our most recent students at McCully District Park: Michelle and Josephine.

Our family: my dad, Eddie Masaki, my husband, Randy Tanaka, and my two sons, Ron and Dustin Tanaka, for their time, effort, and muscles carrying my boxes up and down the stairs every day. And last but not least, my mom May for her humbug leis. I call them humbug leis, but they really are beautiful.

Aunty Lucy, for her help with experimenting with colors and ideas, and her time going to the florist to see actual flower leis.

Kathrine Horikawa, for translating for our students as well as instructing and being there for us.

Happy lei making!
Coryn Tanaka

How to Use This Book

This book is designed for use by both beginning and experienced ribbon lei makers.

The **Supplies** section describes the needles, ribbons, and accessories you will need to make the leis. To be sure you get the right supplies, take this book with you when you go to Flora-Dec. The clerks there are familiar with the ribbons and can answer questions you have about lei-making supplies.

The **Basic Steps** section includes step-by-step instructions (including photographs) explaining the techniques you will use to make the three types of leis included in this book. If you are a beginner, familiarize yourself with these techniques first; then, when you are making a particular lei, you can refer back to these instructions. TIP: Tie 2 or 3 12-inch lengths of ribbon to the top wire of the spiral binding and use them as bookmarks to make it easier to refer to sections you need to review.

Experienced lei-makers can skip the **Basic Steps** section and go directly to the individual lei instructions.

Leis made with the **Plumeria stitch**: Beginners may want to start with leis made with the Plumeria (gathering, or running) stitch (pages 12–15). This stitch is simpler than the Pīkake stitch, and leis made with the Plumeria stitch can be made more quickly than those made by cutting, shredding, pinching, and/or rolling.

Leis made with the **Pīkake stitch**: The Pīkake stitch requires more patience than the Plumeria stitch, but with practice it is soon mastered and produces a variety of life-like leis (pages 16–23).

Leis made from **cut pieces**: These leis (pages 24–42) require some preparation time, but the actual sewing goes quickly. These are the showiest leis, and most often mistaken for real flowers.

A two-sided **Grid** for marking ribbons is provided at the end of the book. Just tear out the page and laminate it.

Any of the leis in *Making Ribbon Leis and Other Gifts of Aloha* and *Making Ribbon Leis 2* can be made in school colors for graduations. A list of school colors for Hawai'i high schools and colleges and selected mainland colleges can be found at http://www.besspress.com/leis/.

Supplies

All supplies can be purchased at or mail-ordered from Flora-Dec Sales, 373 N. Nimitz Highway, Honolulu. Creations by Cleo (on Kaua'i) stocks the recommended supplies. On the Neighbor Islands or outside Hawai'i, call local craft stores to locate ribbons by C & G and Schiff.

❶ Needles

Use Westrim beading needles with a large eye and the EZ Craft Needles pack (both found only at Flora-Dec).

- Use beading needles for leis made with nylon acetate, satin, or polyester chiffon ribbons. The small holes these needles make keep the leis from shifting or settling.
- Beading needles are very fragile. Do not put too much pressure on the needle when you are sewing or it will break and you will have to start all over again.
- Use #6 embroidery needles for leis made with satin acetate ribbons; the holes they make are big enough not to shred the thread, but small enough to keep the leis from settling.
- Use the #3 cotton darner for shredding ribbon.

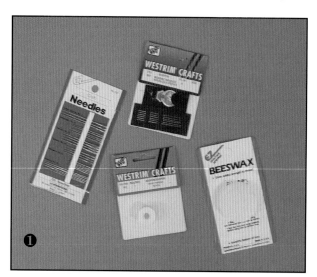

❶ Thread

Use nylon beading thread. Do not use sewing thread, carpet thread, or dental floss.

❶ Beeswax

Beeswax holds the thread together and helps slide the work down.

❷ Wooden Clothespin

The wooden spring clothespin acts as a weight and helps the lei to spin. Plastic clothespins will not work because they are too light.

❷ Marking Pens

Use pens that will not bleed on the ribbons (test first on a small piece of ribbon). Rolling gel pens work best, but other nonbleeding pens are okay (pencils, too, as long as you can see the dots).

❷ Aoyama Tape

Aoyama tape is an all-purpose double-sided tape. Use it to join ribbons that have been cut by the factory (in the middle of the roll). You can also use it to give leis more body or to fix missed stitches (see page 5).

❷ Scissors

Use sharp scissors to avoid shredding the ribbon. Fiskars scallop-edge, mini scallop-edge, and mini ripple scissors, and Fiskars mini pinking shears are used in some leis to replicate petal edges. You can shape the petals with regular scissors, but it will take a long time. Always use scissors, not the Personal Trimmer, when cutting shredded pieces.

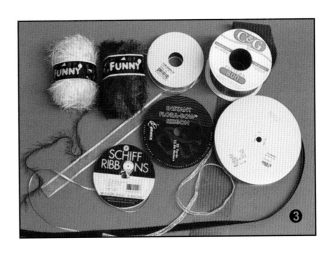

❷ Table Clamp

A table clamp (actually a "bouquet holder"), is optional, but recommended. It acts as a "third hand" to help you shred ribbons, open the petals of some leis, and hold down your work.

Measuring Tape

Use a measuring tape to measure your thread or to check the length of a lei in progress.

Measuring/Marking Grid

Use the grid (pages 43 and 44) to measure and mark your ribbons.

❸ Ribbons and Yarn

Use only C&G, Schiff, and other specific brands of ribbons and yarn mentioned in the instructions. If you use substitutes, the leis may not hold their shape.

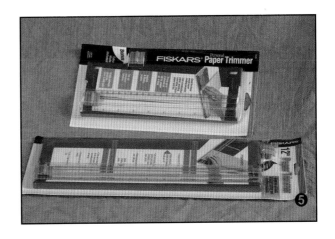

❹ Beads

Some leis use beads of various kinds.

❺ The Fiskars Personal Paper Trimmer and the Fiskars 12" Trimmer are easier to use than scissors as they have built-in rulers, which means you will not have to mark the ribbon first. My instructions assume you are using the paper trimmer instead of scissors. Do not use the trimmer for cutting fringe.

❻ An embroidery floss box or any other container with small compartments is useful for sorting and storing cut pieces.

Basic Steps

Threading

You will need a 3-yard length of thread for each lei. Use a measuring tape or yardstick, or simply pull your thread 2 times, stretching your arms out fully each time.

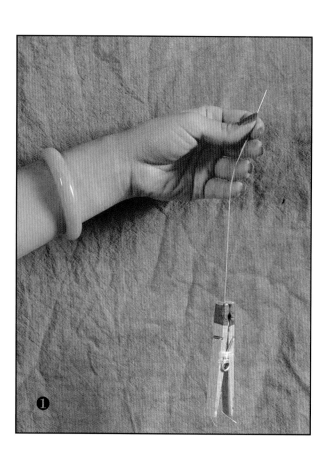

To help keep your thread from knotting, wax your thread (with beeswax or candle wax) before or after threading.

DO NOT use a threader to thread your beading needle; it will fracture the eye and shred your thread.

Thread your needle, double your thread, and tie a knot 3 or 4 inches from the end.

Open your wooden clothespin and slide the knot all the way back to the spring. Close the clothespin and wrap the thread around the clothespin over the spring until about 6 inches remains free.

Tip: If you wind the thread too far back of the spring, the thread will roll off the back of the clothespin. If you wrap it too close to the front, you will not be able to open the clothespin.

❶ Secure the thread between the tips of the clothespin. Placing florist's tape over the inside tips of the clothespin helps prevent the thread from slipping out or shredding.

Make sure your clothespin can turn freely. You can rest it on the table or on your lap while sewing, but when it's time to unwind more thread, you will have to lift it up and away from you and the table.

Marking

❷ Unroll the ribbon from the spool and mark with little dots at the intervals indicated in the instructions for each lei. Use the marking grid on pages 43 and 44. Some leis call for marking down the center of the ribbon; others call for marking along the edge. If you're right-handed, place the spool of ribbon to your left and mark the upper edge of the ribbon; if you're left-handed, place the spool to your right and mark the lower edge.

When sewing two or three different ribbons at a time with different measurements, use different-colored pens to make the dots so you won't get confused.

After you've marked the ribbon, wind it back onto the spool.

Joining

Aoyama Tape

❸ To join two pieces of ribbon (of the same or a different color) place a piece of Aoyama tape across the end of one ribbon, peel off the backing, and attach the other ribbon. Make sure the spacing between the dots stays the same.

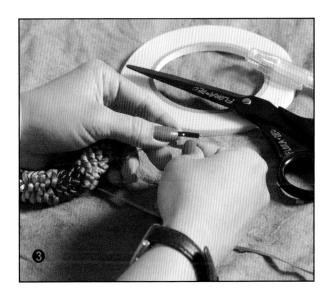

❹ To keep a lei from settling too much, place a small piece of tape over the marked dots at least every two to three yards. It will make your needles sticky, so you'll have to wipe them off occasionally.

To fix a lei if you've accidentally failed to sew through both ribbons when you've taken a stitch, take a small piece of Aoyama tape and place it between the two ribbons as close to the sewn edge as possible.

Stitching

You will use two basic stitches to make the leis: the Plumeria (gathering) stitch and the Pīkake (circular) stitch.

Plumeria (Gathering) Stitch

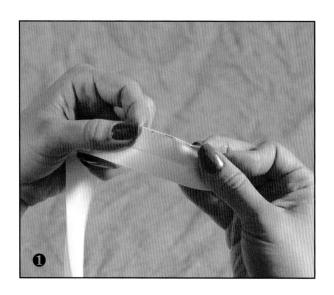

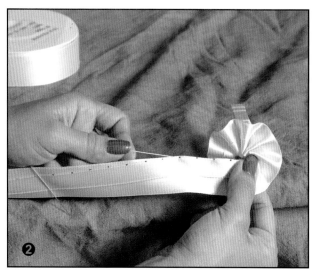

❶ A Plumeria, or gathering, stitch is one that runs along one edge or down the center of the ribbon. Insert your needle through the ribbon at the first dot from underneath, then insert it back though the next dot from the top. Continue sewing from dot to dot. It's okay to gather the ribbon as you sew, but flatten your work after every three or four stitches. Keep the end of the ribbon close to the clothespin.

As the lei gets longer and your thread gets shorter, release just 5 inches of thread from the clothespin and push your work down gently, a little at a time. (If your thread is too long, the ribbon and pin may not turn properly.)

❷ You can form petals every 15 inches or so. That will transform ribbon that looks messy into ribbon that looks like flowers. Connect the clothespin to the table clamp and begin from the bottom of the work, moving upward. Pinch the ribbon along the outside edge and draw it downward as you work the ribbon in a spiral manner around the thread. It will take about 4 pinches to go around the thread one time. Be sure to twist in the same direction with each push. Pulling the thread taut as you do this step will make it easier to slide the ribbon and will make the work neater. When you've neatened all the way to the top, go back to sewing.

Pīkake (Circular) Stitch

❸ A Pīkake stitch is a circular stitch that is always sewn from the underside of the ribbon. Insert your needle at the first dot, from underneath the ribbon. Take your needle around the edge of the ribbon (the right edge if you're right-handed, the left edge if you're left-handed) and up through the next dot. This defines one petal.

Basic Steps

6~

❹ When you make the stitch, rest your clothespin on the table. When you pull the thread, lift the needle, thread, and ribbon so that the clothespin dangles (don't ever hold the clothespin). Pull the thread toward you and the ribbon away from you evenly and slowly. A quickly sewn lei is a messy lei.

❺ Pull the thread and ribbon until nicely shaped cones form—not too tight or the lei will be flat. (Don't try to place the ribbon with your fingers.) The points of the cones should point upward.

❻ If one of your cones is facing down instead of up, release the stitch until you can slip your little finger or your ring finger between the thread and the ribbon. Give the ribbon a little push to turn it in the correct direction.

• Check and correct your work (if necessary) after each stitch. The ribbons have "memories," and the longer the mistake stays in the ribbon, the harder it will be to correct.

Tip: If you don't discover a mistake immediately and need to go back and correct it, don't cut your thread. Pull your thread taut and work the end of your needle through the completed stitches until you get to the mistake. Once the other stitches are off your needle, you can fix your mistake and continue.

• As the lei gets longer and your thread gets shorter, release just 5 inches of thread from the pin and push your work down gently, a little at a time. (If your thread is too long, the ribbon and pin may not turn properly.)

Tip: When you put your work down, secure your needle in a paper napkin or a piece of cloth.

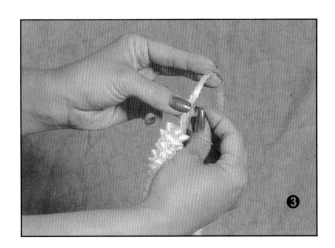

❸

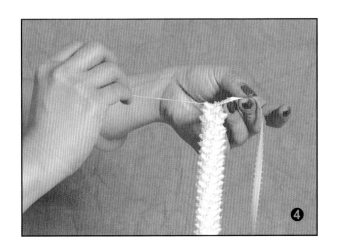

❹

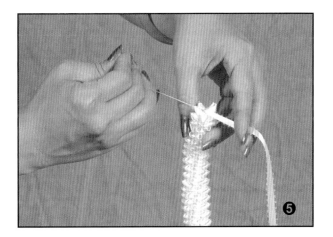

❺

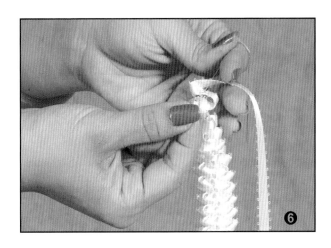

❻

Shredding

If you're a beginner, it may be easier for you to prick and shred one edge of the ribbon at a time. Fold the ribbon in half lengthwise. Unfold. Hold the ribbon flat on the table with your left hand (or your right, if you're left-handed), and with your cotton darner, start in the upper right (or left, if you're left-handed) corner of the ribbon and prick the edge, starting about $1/8$ inch from the edge, to make a fringe. Continue moving downward until you've pricked an inch or two of ribbon.

❶ Starting at the top, grab the threads with your right hand. Hold the ribbon flat on the table with your left hand. Pull straight out (not down), pulling the threads from the ribbon lengthwise.

Continue until you have shredded one edge of the ribbon according to the instructions for each lei. Turn the ribbon around and prick and shred the other edge to match.

❷ A faster way is to hold the ribbon in one hand, with the lengthwise fold toward your palm, and prick and shred both edges at the same time.

❸ When shredding ribbons that will not be cut into smaller pieces, the Long Shred technique is useful. Secure the ribbon with the table clamp about a yard in from the end. Pull the yard-long end taut with one hand and prick and shred the unmarked edge with the other, starting at the end closest to you. Gently pull the threads outward, being sure that they fan open. If you allow the threads to bunch up, they will break off, making it difficult to continue shredding. When you have shredded to the desired width, move the ribbon up another yard and continue.

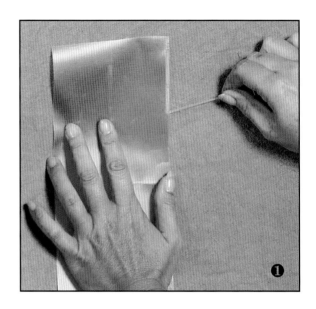

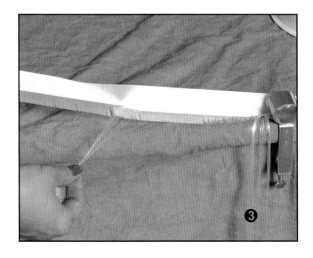

Cutting

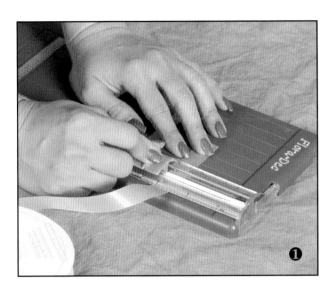

❶ Many leis are made by cutting pieces of ribbon. If you use scissors you will need to mark the ribbon first (see Marking, page 5). If you use the Fiskars Personal Paper Trimmer, you eliminate that step because it has a built-in ruler.

Shredding is used in some leis to make fringe.

❷ Multiple pieces of fringe can be cut without marking. Just make one fold at the measure indicated in the instructions; then accordion fold the rest of the ribbon.

❸ After shredding, cut the ribbon on the accordion folds with scissors (not the Personal Paper Trimmer) so as not to cut the fringe by mistake.

❹ When cutting double-sided fringe into pieces, it's best to refold the ribbon lengthwise and cut from the folded side.

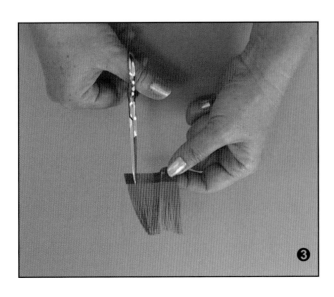

Pinching

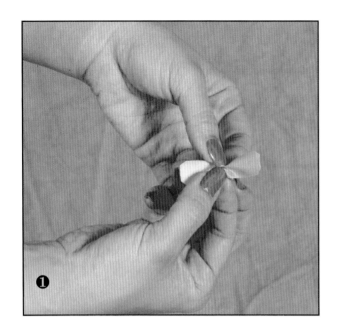

❶ In some leis, short lengths of ribbon are pinched and sewn into the lei. Hold the ribbon with the edges against your thumb and middle finger. With your forefinger, press the middle of the ribbon from underneath slightly while pinching, to form a W-shaped fold. Crease only the center of the ribbon, not all the way to the ends. Insert your needle from the side and sew through the folds to the other side.

Pinching and Folding

❷ To pinch and fold, make a pinch, then fold the ribbon piece in half. Insert your needle from the side and sew through the folds to the other side.

Rolling

❸ Roll (fold without creasing) the piece of ribbon into thirds (so it covers itself halfway). Hold it lightly in the center without creasing. Insert your needle wherever indicated in the instructions. Make sure to insert your needle close to the outside edge.

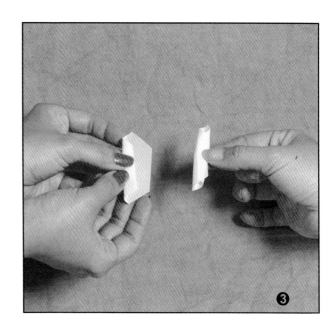

Hanging

All finished leis made with nylon acetate, satin, or polyester chiffon should be hung (vertically, not tied into a circle) with the clothespin at the bottom and the needle at the top. Do not cut anything. Hang the spool of ribbon over the hanger and place another clothespin over the end of the needle and thread.

The lei should hang for a day to settle. If the lei settles more than you expected, add more stitches until it is the length you want. A good finished length for a lei is 38 to 42 inches.

If you are making a lei that you will need right away and won't have time to hang it so it can settle, place a small piece of Aoyama tape over the ribbon markings every two to three yards before you begin sewing.

Tying

❹ After the lei has settled and is the length you want, tie the ends together securely and attach a bow over the knot. A second pair of hands will help to pull the ends together more securely.

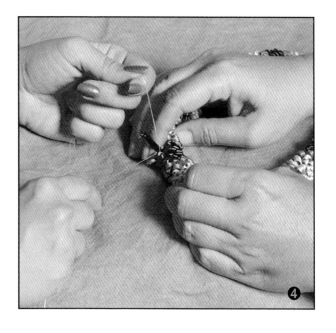

Mini Lehua

designed by Cleo Kana'i of Creations by Cleo

- 20 yards of ³/₈-inch red picot or feather-edge ribbon
- 5 yards of yellow Funny Yarn (so-called "eyebrows")
- 5 yards of orange Funny Yarn
- beading needle
- nylon beading thread
- wooden clothespin
- table clamp

Sew a running stitch in the red picot by inserting your needle at every loop (close to the loops, but not through them) until you reach the end of the available thread. Press the work down, but not too tightly.

❶ You will now transform ribbon that looks messy into ribbon that looks like flowers. I call this "opening the petals." Connect the clothespin to the table clamp and begin from the bottom of the work, moving upward. Pinch the ribbon along the outside edge and draw it downward as you work the ribbon in a spiral manner around the thread. It will take about 4 pinches to go around the thread one time.

Pulling the thread taut as you do this step will make it easier to slide the ribbon and will make the work neater. When you've neatened all the way to the top, go back to sewing.

Repeat until the lei is finished.

❷ After the lei is sewn, and before tying, firmly wind both yarns in the lei's spiral indentation along the entire length of the lei. Be sure to pull the thread taut as you wind.

Finish by tying thread and yarns together tightly.

Option: This lei also looks good as a choker and as a hatband.

Kīkā w/Kukui & Mock Orange

designed by Coryn Tanaka

- 20 yards of C&G #3 ($^1/_2$-inch) Basil ribbon
- 20 yards of $^3/_{16}$-inch Orange picot ribbon or feather-edge ribbon
- 20 yards of $^3/_{16}$-inch Old Gold picot ribbon or feather-edge ribbon
- 18 plastic kukui nut beads
- beading needle
- nylon beading thread
- wooden clothespin
- table clamp
- Fiskars Personal Paper Trimmer

Cut the entire 20 yards of Basil ribbon into 2-inch lengths. Trim each end to a rounded point.

Mark one of the picot ribbons down the center at 1-inch intervals (see page 5). Measure $2^1/_2$ yards of it and cut. Place that ribbon over the other picot ribbon and sew a running stitch, inserting your needle in the dots only.

❶ When you reach the end of the cut ribbon, cut off the end of the back ribbon even with the top ribbon. As you gather the stitches, check the ribbon pattern every so often to make sure all the gathers spiral in the same direction. If you find that some of them have gone the other way, just twist the lei in the opposite direction to straighten it out.

On the table arrange a set of 12 Basil, 1 kukui nut, 12 Basil, 1 kukui nut, 12 Basil, 1 kukui nut, 12 Basil. Pinch a piece of Basil in the center of the ribbon (see Pinching, page 10), being careful not to crease the edges. Sew through the folds. Repeat with the remaining 11 Basil pieces. Add a kukui nut. Continue by sewing alternately through the Basil pieces

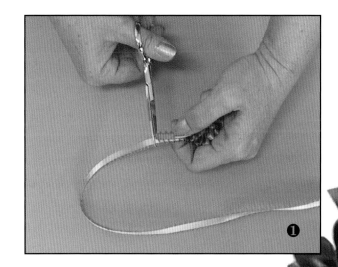

and the kukui nuts and the final group of Basil pieces. You have now completed one section.

Finish the lei by repeating the above steps to add sections until you reach the length you want.

Hawaiian Pansy

designed by May Masaki

- 20 yards of C&G #2 ($^7/_{16}$-inch) Yellow Gold ribbon
- 50 yards of C&G #2 ($^7/_{16}$-inch) Purple ribbon
- 20 yards of Tri-Mar Cleopatra $^5/_8$-inch Purple ribbon
- 50 yards (2 rolls) of Juscotina $^7/_8$-inch Lavender ribbon
- cotton darner
- beading needle
- nylon beading thread
- purple sewing thread
- 3 wooden clothespins
- table clamp

You will make 3 leis separately, then combine them.

Mark the entire Yellow Gold and #2 Purple ribbons every $^5/_{16}$ inches close to one edge on the top side. Shred both ribbons along the edge opposite the marked edge until you have a $^1/_8$ inch band remaining.

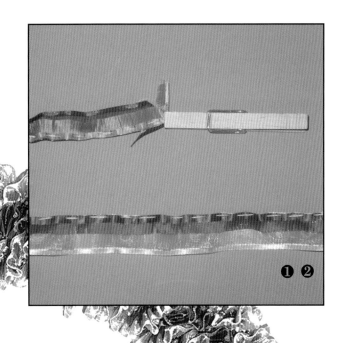

❶ Lei #1: Place the solid edge of the shredded Yellow Gold ribbon on top of one edge of the Cleopatra Purple. Sew a Plumeria stitch through the dots.

Push it down, arrange it firmly so the pattern spirals nicely, and repeat to the end. Put this lei aside.

❷ Lei #2: Place the solid edge of the shredded #2 Purple ribbon on top of one edge of the Juscotina Lavender. Sew a Plumeria stitch through the dots.

Push it down, arrange it firmly so the pattern spirals nicely, and repeat to the end. Cut off the remaining shredded #2 Purple for use in lei #3. Put lei #2 aside.

Lei #3: Place the solid edge of the remaining shredded #2 Purple ribbon on top of one edge of the remaining Juscotina Lavender. Sew a Plumeria stitch through the dots. Push it down firmly, arrange it so the pattern spirals nicely, and repeat to the end. Put this lei aside.

❸ To combine the leis, place the two Lavender leis on the table with the Purple in between. With needle and purple thread, insert the needle through the first Lavender lei, the Purple lei, and the second Lavender lei and out the other side. Pull the thread tight so the outer 2 leis are moved closer together and the middle lei is eased up a bit higher than the other two.

❹ Push the needle one inch up through the center of the second Lavender lei and out.

Push the needle back through the centers of the second Lavender, the Purple, and the first Lavender leis, and out on the first side. Again pull the thread tight so the outer 2 leis are moved closer together and the middle lei is eased up a bit higher than the other two.

Insert the needle one inch up through the center of the first Lavender lei and out.

Repeat sewing as above to the end.

To finish, tie together the 6 threads from both ends. Tie at least 4 tight knots to make it really secure.

Pretty, Easy Bows

- 3 rolls of $1/8$-inch satin ribbon, each roll any color
- needle and thread
- a seed or bugle bead of any color
- wooden clothespin

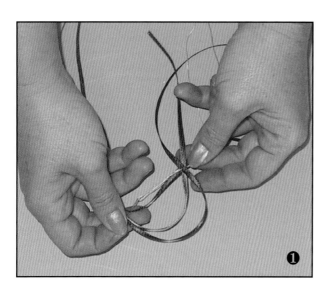

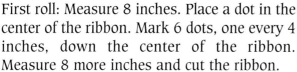

First roll: Measure 8 inches. Place a dot in the center of the ribbon. Mark 6 dots, one every 4 inches, down the center of the ribbon. Measure 8 more inches and cut the ribbon.

Second roll: Measure 6 inches. Place a dot in the center of the ribbon. Mark 6 dots, one every 3 inches, down the center of the ribbon. Measure 6 more inches and cut the ribbon.

Third roll: Measure 4 inches. Place a dot in the center of the ribbon. Mark 6 dots, one every 2 inches, down the center of the ribbon. Measure 4 more inches and cut the ribbon.

Place the ends of the 3 ribbons on top of each other (the one with 2-inch-spaced dots on the bottom, 3-inch in the middle, 4-inch on top), lining up the first dots.

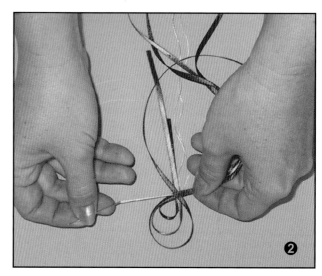

❶ You need only about 8 inches of thread. From the bottom of the ribbons sew through the first dot.

❷ Carefully lining up the dots, sew again from the bottom, forming loops. Repeat to the end of the ribbons.

When the bow is completely sewn, thread the needle through the bead and insert it back through the bow from the top. Tie the thread to the other thread already at the back.

Tip: Use this bow to decorate gift boxes or hairpins with any size bead, button, or ribbon.

Job's Tears

designed by Coryn Tanaka

- 15 yards of C&G #3 ($^1/_2$-inch) Basil ribbon
- 10–12 yards of $^1/_4$-inch Lt. Grey satin ribbon
- 20 plastic kukui nut beads, brown (or any other color)
- crystal rondelle or 4mm faceted crystal bead
- beading needle
- nylon beading thread
- wooden clothespin
- Fiskars Personal Paper Trimmer

Cut the Basil every $1^3/_4$ inches. Trim the ends to a rounded point (like leaf tips).

Mark the back side of the whole roll of Lt. Grey satin ribbon every inch along the edge. Cut it into $2^1/_2$-yard pieces, cutting between the dots.

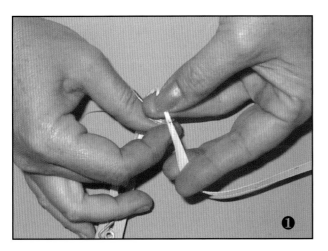

❶ Fold the Lt. Grey ribbon in half lengthwise with the shiny side facing out. Sew a Pīkake Stitch (see page 6) through the folded ribbon (always from the bottom, though the dots only).

Sew 5 petals (5 dots) and place 1 bead. Continue sewing another 5 petals and place another bead. Continue doing the same thing until the $2^1/_2$ yards of ribbon is finished. Don't worry if the last few dots don't make 5 petals. Do not put a bead after the last petals.

Lay out 12 Basil pieces, 1 kukui nut, 12 Basil pieces, 1 kukui nut, 12 Basil pieces. Pinch a Basil piece in the center and sew through the folds (see Pinching, page 10). Repeat with the remaining 11 Basil pieces. Add one kukui nut. Pinch and sew the next 12 Basil pieces, add the kukui nut, and finish with the last 12 Basil pieces. You have now finished 1 set.

You will need 5 or 6 sets, depending on the length you want.

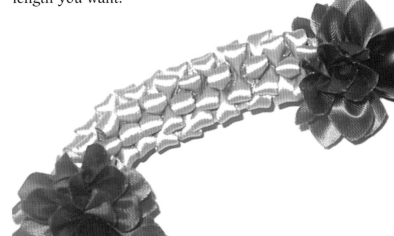

ʻĀkulikuli

designed by Coryn Tanaka

- 60 yards (2 rolls) of $^1/_8$-inch Fuchsia polyester satin ribbon
- 60 yards (2 rolls) of $^1/_8$-inch Moss polyester satin ribbon
- 20 yards of C&G #5 ($^7/_8$-inch) Cyclamen satin acetate ribbon
- beading needle
- nylon beading thread
- wooden clothespin
- beeswax

Pīkake Stitch and Cut Pieces

Mark the Fuchsia ribbon down the center every $1^1/_2$ inches. Mark the Moss down the center every inch.

Mark the Cyclamen ribbon at $1^1/_2$ inches and fold. Using this as a measure, continue folding the entire Cyclamen ribbon back and forth, accordion style (see page 9). Open it up and shred it along one side until you have a $^1/_8$-inch band remaining (see page 8). Cut the ribbon along the folds.

Wax the thread. Place the clothespin at the knot. You will be sewing a Pīkake Stitch (see page 6) using a long thread, so be very careful not to tangle the thread.

Place the Fuchsia ribbon on top of the Moss ribbon. Stitch 6 times from the underside, carefully matching up the dots.

❶ Place a Cyclamen piece on your needle and sew a small running stitch down the narrow band of unshredded ribbon, twisting it on the

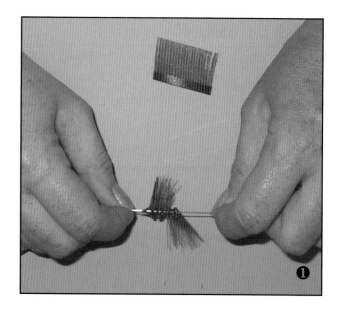

needle so it spirals all the way around. Bring it down to your work. (Be careful, as the needle is thin and could break.)

Next sew 5 Pīkake stitches and 1 Cyclamen fringe, as above. Then sew 7 Pīkake stitches and a Cyclamen fringe. Rewax your thread. (Waxing holds the thread together and helps slide the work down.)

❷ Continue repeating this pattern (6 Pīkake stitches, 1 fringe, 5 Pīkake stitches, 1 fringe, 7 Pīkake stitches, 1 fringe). It's okay if the fringe does not open fully, but it shouldn't clump. Be sure to pack your work down tightly from the center by the thread.

When you run out of each first roll of polyester satin ribbon, attach the second with Aoyama tape (see page 5).

Note: This lei takes a lot of time and concentration. It is not for beginners.

This lei looks good twisted with another 'Ākulikuli or with one Pīkake.

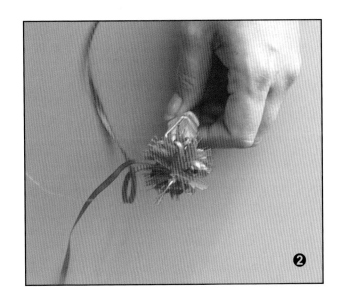

Pīkake stitch

Snowflake

designed by Coryn Tanaka

- 50 yards of $3/16$-inch White picot or feather-edge ribbon
- 2 rolls (25 yards each roll) of Berwick White iridescent Instant Flora-bow ribbon
- 5 yards of C&G #40 ($2^1/_2$-inch) White acetate ribbon
- 1 skein metallic silver embroidery floss
- beading needle
- nylon beading thread
- wooden clothespin
- cotton darner
- beeswax
- Fiskars Personal Paper Trimmer

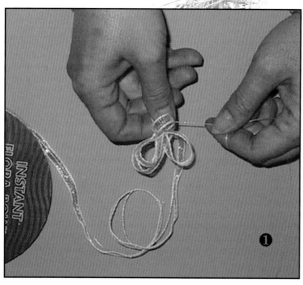

the ink will go through because it's made with woven plastic; so mark the edge.

Mark the White acetate ribbon at 2 inches. Fold back and forth accordion-fashion (see page 9). Open it and refold it in half lengthwise. From the open sides of the ribbon start shredding the ribbon (see page 8) till you have about a half-inch band in the middle (or roughly $1/_4$ inch on each side of the fold). Cut the ribbon at every 2-inch fold, then cut each piece in half to make one-inch pieces, and in half again to make $1/_2$-inch pieces.

Mark the White picot ribbon at 1-inch intervals down the center of the ribbon (see page 5).

❶ Pull out the center thread from both rolls of the iridescent instant bow.

Mark the edge of the iridescent ribbon every $1^1/_2$ inches. If you mark the center of this ribbon (which is actually where you will sew it),

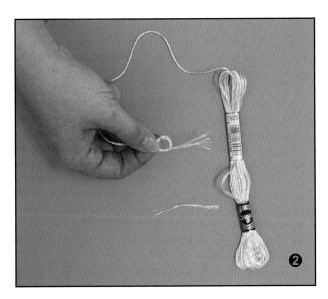

❷ Tie a knot two inches from the end of the metallic floss. Cut off two inches above the knot to make a 4-inch piece with a knot in the middle. Repeat until the skein is used up.

Place the iridescent ribbon on top of the picot ribbon. Line up the first dots and stitch from the bottom of the ribbons (see Pīkake Stitch, page 6). Note: although you have marked the iridescent ribbon on the edge, you will line up and sew through the centers of both ribbons.

Continue lining up the dots for the two ribbons, always stitching from the bottom. Each stitch forms a loop that looks like a petal. (Note: the inner ribbon will have a smaller loop than the outer.) Stitch 5 petals.

Add 1 white fringe by sewing a small running stitch down the middle of the ribbon and pressing it down to the petals. Add one floss element by stitching through the knot.

Continue repeating the above steps until you come to the end of the iridescent ribbon. Join it to the next iridescent ribbon with a small piece of Aoyama tape (see page 5). Continue sewing until the lei is the length you prefer.

Pīkake Stitch and Cut Pieces

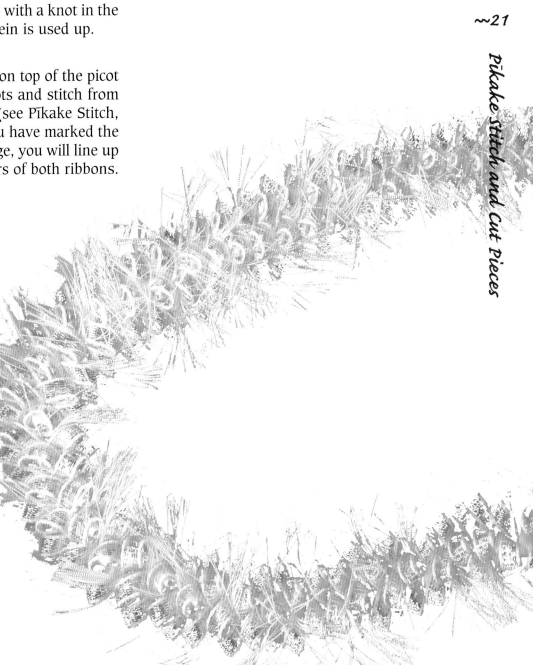

Crownflower with Bozu

designed by Aunty Lucy, revised by Coryn Tanaka

- 60 yards (2 rolls) of $^1/_8$-inch Lt. Grey satin ribbon
- 60 yards (2 rolls) of $^1/_8$-inch Purple satin ribbon
- 5 yards of C&G #3 ($^1/_2$-inch) Basil acetate ribbon
- beading needle
- nylon beading thread
- 2 wooden clothespins
- beeswax
- table clamp
- Fiskars Personal Paper Trimmer

Pīkake Stitch and Cut Pieces

Mark the Lt. Grey ribbon down the center every $1^1/_2$ inches. Measure 4 yards and cut the ribbon.

Mark 30 yards of the first roll of Purple ribbon every inch down the center. Do not cut it off until you have sewn it.

Mark 30 yards of the second Purple down the center of the ribbon as follows: 18 dots at $^3/_4$ inch, 23 dots at 1 inch, 12 dots at $^3/_4$ inch, and 6 dots at $^5/_8$ inch. Cut the ribbon $^1/_8$ inch after the last $^5/_8$-inch dot. You will need a total of 18 of these variably marked sections.

Cut 2 yards of the Basil into 1-inch pieces and the remainder into $1^3/_4$-inch pieces. Trim the ends to a rounded point that looks like a leaf tip.

Wax your thread and wind it around the clothespin until you have about 6 inches from your needle to the clothespin.

Place the cut 4-yard piece of Lt. Grey on top of the 1-inch marked Purple ribbon. Sew them together with a Pīkake stitch, always inserting the needle from the bottom of the ribbon. Be careful to match the dots. Continue until you reach the end of the Lt. Grey ribbon. Cut the Purple ribbon.

Unwind the thread from the clothespin, leaving the knot in place. Attach the clothespin to the table clamp. Push the Lt. Grey and Purple crownflower down to the bottom of the thread.

❶ Loosen or adjust the ribbon so that the Purple is visible in the center of the Lt. Grey. Rewax the thread. This completes the first crownflower section.

❷ Pinch the thread with the second clothespin about 6 inches from the needle. Lay out 2 $1^3/_4$-inch pieces of Basil and 2 1-inch pieces of Basil. Pinch and sew a $1^3/_4$-inch Basil piece through the folds (see Pinching, page 10). Repeat with another $1^3/_4$-inch piece of Basil, then a 1-inch piece and another 1-inch piece. Starting at the $^3/_4$-inch end of the Purple ribbon with the variable markings, sew Pīkake

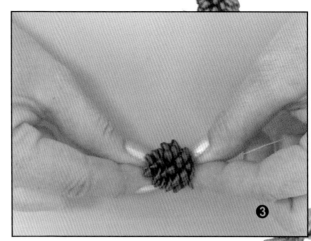

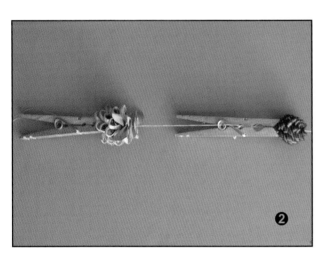

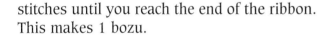

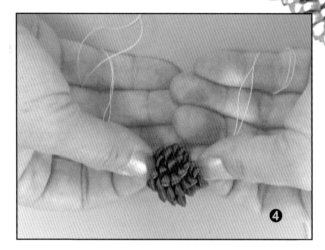

stitches until you reach the end of the ribbon. This makes 1 bozu.

Now you will compress the bozu to give it a nice round shape.

❸ Push the bozu together while holding on to the thread from both sides of the flower and pushing toward the center with both thumbs and index fingers.

❹ To compress it further, wrap both ends of the thread around your pinky fingers, pinch the thread on both sides of the flower, and again push toward the center. Note: if you compress the flower by just pushing it down instead of pushing it toward its center, the shape will not come out right.

Open the top clothespin and push the first bozu and leaf down till you reach the crown-flower. Don't push the bozu on top of the

crownflower too tightly. Place it so it's just sitting on top. Adjust the bozu so it has a proper round shape.

Pinch a piece of 1-inch Basil ribbon in the center and sew it through the folds. Repeat with a second piece. Move the clothespin back to the top, about 6 inches from the needle, and sew another purple bozu as described above. Pinch a piece of $1^3/_4$-inch Basil ribbon in the center and sew it through the folds. Repeat with a second piece. Open the top clothespin and slide everything down, but not too tightly or the lei will look smashed. That is one set.

Place the clothespin back at the top and make about 8 more sets.

Note: This is a beautiful lei, but it will take time to make. So be patient.

Ōla'a Beauty

designed by Coryn Tanaka

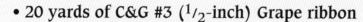

- 20 yards of C&G #3 ($^1/_2$-inch) Grape ribbon
- 20 yards of C&G #3 ($^1/_2$-inch) Plum ribbon
- 20 yards of C&G #3 ($^1/_2$-inch) New Violet ribbon
- 20 yards of C&G #3 ($^1/_2$-inch) Belle ribbon
- #6 embroidery needle
- nylon beading thread
- wooden clothespin
- table clamp
- Fiskars Personal Paper Trimmer

24～

Cut Pieces

Cut the Grape ribbon every 2 inches and trim both ends into half-circles. Cut the Plum every $1^3/_4$ inches and trim the ends into half-circles. Cut the New Violet ribbon every $1^1/_4$ inches and clip off the tips of the corners. Cut the Belle ribbon every inch and clip off the tips of the corners.

Set out 2 Grape pieces, 2 Plum pieces, 2 New Violet pieces, and 2 Belle pieces. Pinch and sew a piece of Grape through the folds (see Pinching, page 10). Do the same with the second piece of Grape; then a Plum piece and another Plum piece.

❶ Now place one piece of Belle on top of a piece of New Violet, both shiny-side up. Pinch them together and sew through the folds. Do the same with the remaining pair. Don't line up the petals as you are sewing; place them randomly.

Gently push all the pieces down to the clothespin. The lei should be flexible, but the thread should not show.

Repeat for the rest of the lei.

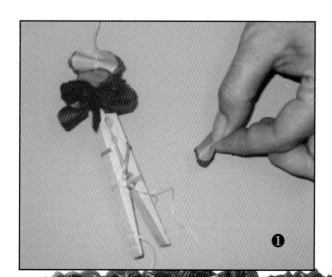
❶

Firecracker

designed by Aunty Lucy

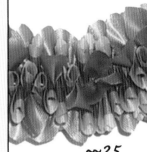

20 yards of C&G #5 ($^7/_8$-inch) Orange ribbon

• 20 yards of C&G #5 ($^7/_8$-inch) Belle ribbon

• 20 yards of C&G #3 ($^1/_2$-inch) Basil ribbon

• Fiskars scallop-edge scissors (purple handle)

• #6 embroidery needle

• nylon beading thread

• wooden clothespin

• table clamp

• Fiskars Personal Paper Trimmer

Cut Pieces

Cut the Orange ribbon every inch and the Belle ribbon every 1$^1/_2$ inches. Trim both ends of the Belle with the scallop-edge scissors. Cut the Basil every 1$^3/_4$ inches and trim the ends to a rounded point (like a leaf tip).

❶ Center 1 piece of Orange on top of 1 piece of Belle with the shiny sides up. Roll into thirds (both ends over the middle segment). Do not crease. Insert the needle through the center of the overlaps from the bottom. Add 2 more pairs of orange and belle in the same way. This completes the firecracker segment.

❷ Pinch the center of a piece of Basil ribbon and sew through the creases (see Pinching, page 10). Repeat with another Basil piece.

Continue alternating the firecracker segments and the leaves until you finish the lei.

Note: Make this lei a little tight, but not so tight that the ends smash. A good way to test it is to hold the ends of the lei together, and look at the bottom center. It should fall nicely into a graceful curve.

Kukui nuts look good spaced along this lei.

❶

❷

Mini Carnation

designed by Aunty Lucy

- 20 yards of C&G #5 ($^7/_8$-inch) Pink ribbon (or any other color)
- 20 yards of C&G #5 ($^7/_8$-inch) Red ribbon (or any other color)
- 20 yards of C&G #3 ($^1/_2$-inch) Basil ribbon
- 1 red tri bead
- 1 pink tri bead
- Fiskars mini scallop-edge scissors (mustard handle)
- #6 embroidery needle
- nylon beading thread
- wooden clothespin
- beeswax
- table clamp
- Fiskars Personal Paper Trimmer

Cut off 11 yards of the Pink and the Red ribbons. Cut these ribbons into $1^3/_4$-inch segments. Cut the rest of the 2 ribbons into $1^1/_2$-inch pieces. Trim both ends of the pieces with the mini scallop-edge scissors. Cut the Basil ribbon into $1^1/_4$-inch pieces. Trim the ends to a rounded point (like a leaf tip).

Wax the thread. Place the clothespin at the knot and attach it to the table clamp. Place 4 pieces of Basil, 8 pieces of $1^3/_4$-inch Pink, 6 pieces of $1^1/_2$-inch Pink, and 1 pink tri bead on the table.

Pinch one piece of Basil in the center and sew through the folds (see Pinching, page 10). Repeat with all the Basil you set out, all the 1 $^3/_4$-inch Pinks, all the remaining Pink pieces and the bead.

❶ Grab one end of the thread in each hand. Compress the flower from both sides by using your thumbs and index fingers to push. To compress it further wrap the ends of the thread around your pinky fingers, pinch the thread on both sides of the flower, and again push toward the center (see page 23). That's one carnation. If you compress the flower by just pushing it down instead of pushing it toward its center, the shape will not come out round.

Bring the flower down to the bottom of your thread.

Do the same thing for the other color. Repeat from the top until you finish your lei.

Dendrobium

designed by Coryn Tanaka

- 5 yards of C&G #5 ($^7/_8$-inch) Ivory
- 20 yards of C&G #3 ($^1/_2$-inch) Ivory
- 20 yards of C&G #3 ($^1/_2$-inch) Eggshell
- 1 yard of C&G #3 ($^1/_2$-inch) Purple
- 4mm faceted dark amethyst bead
- Fiskars mini scallop-edge scissors (mustard handle)
- #6 embroidery needle
- nylon beading thread
- wooden clothespin
- table clamp
- Fiskars Personal Paper Trimmer

Cut the #5 Ivory, #3 Ivory, and the Eggshell into 2-inch pieces. Cut the Purple into 1$^1/_4$-inch pieces. Trim the ends of the Ivory and Eggshell pieces to a rounded dome shape. Use the mini scallop-edge scissors to trim both ends of the Purple pieces.

Set out 1 #3 Ivory, 1 #5 Ivory, 2 Eggshell, 1 Purple, 1 bead. Pinch (see Pinching, page 10) the centers of each ribbon and sew through the folds. When you reach the Purple ribbon, pinch and fold it in half and sew through the stub (see Pinching and Folding, page 10).

❶ Now go back and twist one petal of the #5 Ivory so it lies at a right angle with the opposite petal. ❷ Arrange the Purple petal so it lines up with the end of the petal you just twisted. Place a bead. This makes one flower.

Now you will compress the flower to give it a nice, round shape. Push all the petals together while holding on to the thread from both sides of the flower and pushing toward the center with both thumbs and index fingers.

To compress it further wrap the ends of the thread around your pinky fingers, pinch the thread on both sides of the flower, and again push toward the center (see photo, page 26). Note: If you compress the flower by just pushing it down instead of pushing it toward its center, the shape will not come out right.

Each flower should be pressed down lightly over the previous one.

Repeat until all pieces are sewn.

❶

Pink ʻŌhai Aliʻi

designed by Coryn Tanaka

- 20 yards of C&G #3 ($^1/_2$-inch) Bermuda Pink ribbon
- 20 yards of C&G #3 ($^1/_2$-inch) R. Pink ribbon
- 5 yards of C&G #3 ($^1/_2$-inch) Yellow ribbon
- 2 yards of C&G #100 (4-inch) Azalea ribbon
- #6 embroidery needle
- nylon beading thread
- wooden clothespin
- table clamp
- Fiskars Personal Paper Trimmer

Note: There are 3 ʻŌhai Aliʻi in this book. Each one is made differently.

Cut the Bermuda Pink and R. Pink ribbons into 1$^1/_2$-inch pieces. Clip off the tips of the 4 corners, leaving the tops and bottoms flat. Cut the Yellow ribbon into 1-inch pieces and clip off the tips of all the corners.

Fold the Azalea ribbon 2 inches up from the end. Using this as a measure, fold back and forth, accordion style (see page 9). Open and refold lengthwise. Shred according to the instructions on page 8 until you have a $^1/_2$-inch band remaining in the center of the ribbon ($^1/_4$ inch on each side of the fold). Cut on the accordion folds with scissors, working from the lengthwise fold. Cut each piece in half with scissors to make 1-inch pieces.

Place 2 pieces of Bermuda Pink, 2 pieces of R. Pink, 2 pieces of Yellow, and 1 fringe on the table. Pinch each piece in the center of the ribbon (see Pinching, page 10) and sew through the folds. Continue until you reach the fringe.

❶ Open the fringe up and sew a small running stitch down the center of the ribbon. Press it down to the clothespin. This makes one flower.

Continue creating more flowers until the lei is the length you like.

Orange 'Ōhai Ali'i

designed by May Masaki

- 20 yards of C&G #3 ($1/_2$-in.) Orange ribbon
- 20 yards of C&G #3 ($1/_2$-inch) Valeria ribbon
- 20 yards of C&G #3 ($1/_2$-inch) Belle ribbon
- 5 yards of C&G #100 (4-inch) Red ribbon
- cotton darner
- Fiskars mini pinking shears (orange handle)
- #6 embroidery needle
- nylon beading thread
- wooden clothespin
- table clamp
- Fiskars Personal Paper Trimmer

Cut off 6 yards of Orange ribbon and trim into $1^1/_2$-inch pieces. Cut off 12 yards more and trim into $1^3/_4$-inch pieces. Use the rest as needed. Do the same with the Valeria. Cut the Belle into 2-inch pieces.

Fold the Red ribbon 2 inches up from the end. Using this as a measure, fold, accordion style (see page 9). Open and refold lengthwise. Shred (see page 8) until you have a $1/_2$-inch band in the middle ($1/_4$ inch on each side of the fold). Cut on the accordion folds. Cut each piece in half with scissors to make 1-inch pieces. Cut those pieces into thirds.

Trim the $1^3/_4$-inch Orange and Valeria pieces by clipping off the tips of the 4 corners, leaving the tops and bottoms flat. Trim the $1^1/_2$-inch Orange to a rounded dome shape.

❶ Trim both ends of the 2-inch Belle and the $1^1/_2$-inch Valeria with the mini pinking shears, cutting off the corners to form a point.

Lay out the following piles to make one flower: 2 Orange $1^3/_4$-inch pieces; 2 Valeria 1 $3/_4$-inch pieces; 2 Orange $1^3/_4$-inch pieces; 1 Valeria $1^1/_2$-inch piece, 1 Belle, and 1 Orange $1^1/_2$-inch piece (these 3 pieces to be sewn together); and 1 fringe.

Pinch each piece in the center (see page 10) and sew through the folds. Bring each petal down to the table clamp by pushing along the thread. Continue this, using up all the pieces in the above order. Pinch and sew the Valeria/Belle/Orange combination with the Valeria and Orange pieces shiny side out. Sew the fringe piece with a small running stitch down the center. Arrange the pieces randomly so they don't stack up on top of each other.

Repeat until the lei is finished.

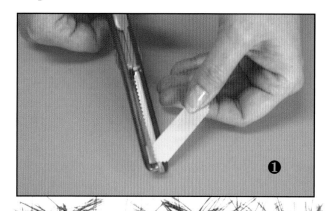

❶

Purple 'Ōhai Ali'i

designed by May Masaki

- 20 yards of C&G #3 ($1/_2$-inch) Purple ribbon
- 20 yards of C&G #3 ($1/_2$-inch) Lavender ribbon
- 10 yards of Flora Satin $5/_8$-inch Lavender ribbon
- 10 yards of C&G #3 ($1/_2$-inch) Yellow ribbon
- 20 yards of C&G #3 ($1/_2$-inch) Violet ribbon
- 1 1/2 yards of C&G #100 (4-inch) Purple ribbon
- 3 yards of C&G #9 ($1^1/_4$-inch) White ribbon
- Fiskars mini ripple-edge scissors (green handle)
- cotton darner
- #6 embroidery needle
- nylon beading thread
- wooden clothespin
- table clamp
- Fiskars Personal Paper Trimmer

Cut the #3 Purple ribbon, the #3 Lavender ribbon, and the Flora Satin Lavender ribbon into $1^3/_4$-inch pieces. Cut the Yellow ribbon into $1^1/_4$-inch pieces. Cut 14 yards of the Violet into $1^3/_4$-inch pieces and 5 yards of the Violet into 1-inch pieces. Use the remainder as needed.

Fold the #100 Purple ribbon 2 inches up from the end. Using this as a measure, fold back and forth, accordion style (see page 9). Open and refold lengthwise. Shred according to the instructions on page 8 until you have a $1/_2$-inch band remaining in the center of the ribbon ($1/_4$ inch on each side of the fold). Cut on the accordion folds with scissors, working from the lengthwise fold. Cut each piece in half with scissors to make 1-inch pieces, again to make $1/_2$-inch pieces, then again to make $1/_4$-inch pieces.

Fold the White ribbon 2 inches up from the end. Using this as a measure, fold back and forth, accordion style. Open and shred the White ribbon until you have a 1/4-inch band remaining at one edge. With scissors, cut the ribbon on the accordion folds; then cut each piece in half to make 1-inch pieces.

Pinch and sew each petal in the center. (See Pinching, page 10).

When you reach the Yellow and Violet ribbon pair, place the Violet ribbon on top of the Yellow with both shiny surfaces facing up.

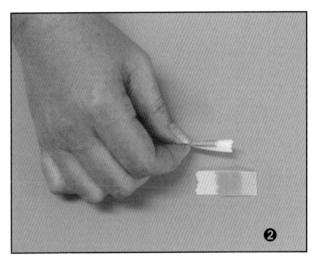

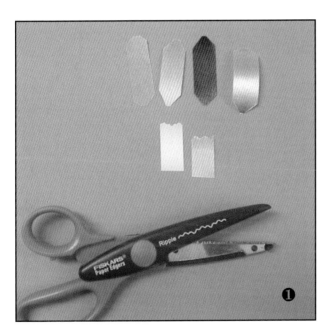

❶ Trim the cut Purple, Violet, Lavender, and Flora Satin Lavender pieces by clipping off the tips of the corners, leaving the tops and bottoms flat. These pieces are the petals. With the Fiskars mini ripple-edge scissors, trim one end of the Yellow pieces and the Violet pieces.

Lay out one flower set: 1 Purple piece, 2 Violet pieces, 2 Lavender pieces, 1 Flora Satin Lavender piece, 1 Purple piece, 1 Yellow piece with 1 Violet piece (to be sewn together), 1 Purple fringe, 1 White fringe.

❷ Roll the two together (see Rolling, page 11) and sew through the untrimmed edge (tops will flare slightly open).

Unfold the Purple fringe piece flat and sew a running stitch down the center. Do the same for the White fringe piece, but sewing down the edge of the band.

Check that the pieces have been placed randomly and do not line up directly over each other. Bring your work down to the table clamp. You have now made one flower.

Repeat the above 4 paragraphs for the entire length of the lei.

Lokelani

designed by Coryn Tanaka

- 20 yards of C&G #9 ($1\frac{1}{4}$-inch) Azalea ribbon
- 20 yards of C&G #9 ($1\frac{1}{4}$-inch) Forever Yours ribbon
- 20 yards of C&G #9 ($1\frac{1}{4}$-inch) Basil ribbon
- 5 yards of C&G #40 ($2\frac{1}{2}$-inch) Belle ribbon
- 5 yards of C&G #40 ($2\frac{1}{2}$-inch) Orange ribbon
- Fiskars scallop-edge scissors (purple handle)
- cotton darner needle
- #6 embroidery needle
- nylon beading thread
- wooden clothespin
- table clamp
- Fiskars Personal Paper Trimmer

Cut the Azalea, Forever Yours, and Basil ribbons into $1\frac{1}{2}$-inch pieces.

❶ Shape one side (not end) of each piece into a dome shape using the scallop-edge scissors. Leave about $\frac{1}{2}$-inch of flat, uncut surface on the ends.

Cut off 2 yards of the Orange ribbon. Fold it up 2 inches from the end. Using this as a measure, fold back and forth, accordion style (see page 9). Open and refold lengthwise. Shred (see page 8) from the sides of the ribbon until $\frac{1}{2}$ inch remains down the center ($\frac{1}{4}$ inch on each side of the fold). Cut on the 2-inch folds, then cut again to make 1-inch pieces.

Do the same with the Belle ribbon.

To form the Basil and Azalea pieces into cone shapes before sewing them into the lei:

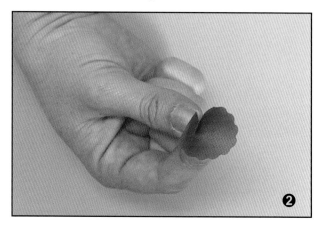

❷ Place one piece of Basil on the table with the long flat side toward you and the wrong side up. Fold the right half of the base up

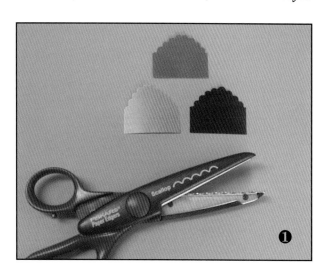

❶

across the ribbon at a 45-degree angle. Then fold up the other side to cover it. Press the bottom half of the sides (be careful not to crease all the way up; it should have a rounded cone shape). Fold all the Basil pieces.

Place one piece of Azalea in front of you with the long flat side toward you and the wrong side up. Fold in half from left to right, creasing the bottom half of the fold only.

❸ Unfold and then fold in the corners so the two halves of the bottom edge meet at the center crease. Next, fold the piece in half along the center crease to form a cone shape. Tip: be careful not to flatten the tops of the cones, as they need to flare out at the tops. Fold all the Azalea pieces.

Fold the Forever Yours pieces the same as the Azalea pieces.

Now you're ready to assemble the lei. Place 5 Basil, 12 Azalea, 1 Orange fringe and 1 Belle fringe (to be sewn together), 5 Basil, 12 Forever Yours, 1 Orange fringe and 1 Belle fringe (to be sewn together) in that order in front of you.

❹ For the cone pieces, insert your needle about $1/4$ inch up from the point.

Place the 2 fringe pieces together, sew a running stitch up the solid center, and then twist the fringe on the needle so the fringe takes on a spiral shape (see photo, page 18).

❺ As you slide each piece down, arrange it so it overlaps the previous one just a bit. The pieces will spiral around the thread.

Continue with the remaining sets of ribbon.

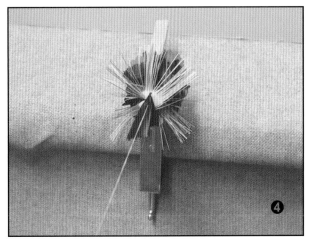

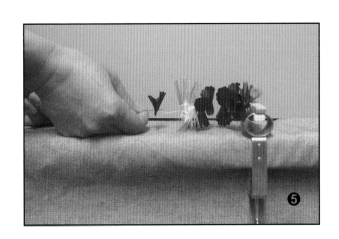

Yellow Mum

designed by May Masaki

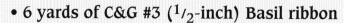

- 6 yards of C&G #3 ($^1/_2$-inch) Basil ribbon
- 50 yards of C&G #2 ($^7/_{16}$-inch) Belle ribbon
- 40 yards of C&G #2 ($^7/_{16}$-inch) R. Gold ribbon
- 1 bag of 6mm faceted crystal beads
- #6 embroidery needle
- nylon beading thread
- wooden clothespin
- table clamp
- Fiskars Personal Paper Trimmer

Cut Pieces

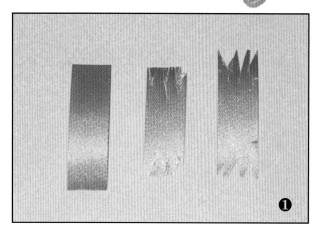

❶ Cut the entire length of the Basil every 1 $^3/_4$ inches. Trim both ends to make irregular, sharply pointed vees. This is for the calyx.

Cut 25 yards of the Belle every 3 inches and 20 yards every 2$^1/_2$ inches, leaving about 5 yards uncut. Use this as needed.

Cut all 40 yards of R. Gold at 1$^3/_4$ inches.

Attach the knot with a 3-inch tail to the clothespin, leaving the thread unwrapped. Attach the clothespin to the table clamp. This means you will have to work with a very long thread, but the lei will come out better than if you work in smaller sections that repeatedly get pushed down.

Lay out 3 pieces of Basil, 8 pieces of 3-inch Belle, 16 pieces of 2$^1/_2$-inch Belle, 12 pieces of R. Gold, and 1 bead.

Pinch a Basil piece in the center (see Pinching, page 10) and stitch through the side. Repeat with the other 2 pieces of Basil.

❷ With the dull side up, fold a 3-inch Belle piece in half end to end. Unfold and twist hard two times so the dull side returns to the top. Fold the petal on the twist so that the shiny side is facing out.

❸ Holding both ends together with both hands, pinch and press your fingers together to make 2 tiny folds in the ends only. (The fold will have a Z shape.) Sew through the folds. Continue doing the same for the rest of the 3-inch Belle pieces.

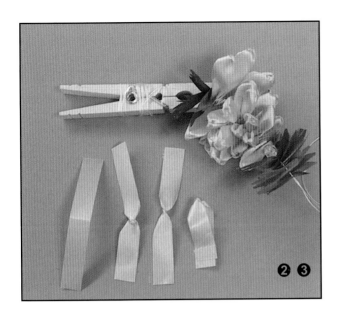

❹ Press the Basil leaves down and fan them out so they extend all the way around the thread.

Firmly press the 3-inch Belle pieces down, fanning them around the thread.

Now sew a 2$^1/_2$-inch Belle piece as you did the 3-inch Belle, and firmly press it down.

Continue in the same manner with each of the remaining pieces of Belle and R. Gold you've set out.

❺ Press down hard from the center of the flower along the thread. Add the bead. This makes one flower.

Keep on making flowers until the lei is long enough.

(Back in the '60s when ribbon flowers were popular, May made this flower as part of a floral arrangement along with sprays of ribbon roses. She still has it on top of the organ. She decided to make it into a lei around 1995.)

Petite Blue Ginger

designed by Coryn Tanaka

- 50 yards of C&G #5 ($^7/_8$-inch) Periwinkle ribbon (1 roll)
- 20 yards of C&G #3 ($^1/_2$-inch) Purple ribbon
- 20 yards of C&G #3 ($^1/_2$-inch) Fuchsia ribbon
- 20 yards of C&G #9 ($1^1/_4$-inch) Yellow ribbon
- 1 yards of C&G #40 ($1^1/_4$-inch) White ribbon
- cotton darner
- #6 embroidery needle
- nylon beading thread
- wooden clothespin
- table clamp
- Fiskars Personal Paper Trimmer

❶ Cut the entire roll of the Periwinkle ribbon into $1^1/_2$-inch pieces. To shape the ends, fold each piece in half lengthwise (don't crease the fold). With the fold held vertically, cut up from the bottom of the fold at a 45-degree angle. Reverse the piece and clip the other end in the same way. When you open it up, you will see a 6-sided piece with each side about the same length.

Cut the Purple and the Fuchsia ribbons into 2-inch pieces. Clip off the tips of the 4 corners.

Fold the Yellow at 2 inches. Using this as a measure, fold it back and forth, accordian style (see page 9). Open it up and refold it in half lengthwise. Do the Long Shred a yard at a time (see page 8) until you have a $^1/_2$-inch center panel ($^1/_4$ inch on each side of the fold). Release and start again with the next yard

until you have reached the end. Cut the ribbon with scissors on the folds. Cut again to make 1-inch-long pieces.

Cut 1 yard of White ribbon and treat it as you did the Yellow ribbon. Cut the White pieces in half another time to make $^1/_2$-inch pieces.

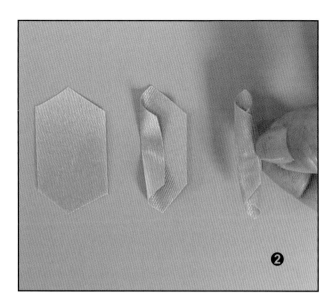

Prepare 20 sets of 6 Periwinkle and 1 Yellow fringe.

❷ Roll the sides of one piece of the Periwinkle loosely into thirds with the shiny side facing out. Hold by the center only, so the ends will stay rounded.

Sew the petal exactly through the middle. Bring it down to the table clamp by pushing only in the center. Sew a small running stitch down the center of the Yellow fringe; then twist it all the way around the needle (see photo, page 18). Push it down to the clamp. Don't worry if it doesn't stay in a full circle. Do the same for all the sets.

Lay out 8 pieces of Purple, 4 pieces of Fuchsia, and 1 White fringe.

Pinch and fold (see Pinching and Folding, page 10) each piece of Purple ribbon. Repeat with the Fuchsia ribbon. Sew a small running stitch down the center of the White fringe to complete this set.

Continue adding these alternating sets until the lei is fnished.

Cut Pieces

Twisty Cigar

designed by Aunty Lucy, revised by Coryn Tanaka

- 20 yards of C&G #5 ($^7/_8$-inch) Brown ribbon
- 10 yards of C&G #5 ($^7/_8$-inch) Orange ribbon
- 20 yards of C&G #3 ($^1/_2$-inch) Basil ribbon
- 1 yard of C&G #100 (4-inch) Basil ribbon
- 18 to 20 plastic kukui nut beads

Fiskars mini scallop-edge scissors (mustard handle)
- cotton darner
- #6 embroidery needle
- nylon beading thread
- 2 wooden clothespins
- table clamp
- Fiskars Personal Paper Trimmer

Cut off 5 yards of Brown ribbon. Fold it at 2 inches. Using this as a measure, accordion fold the entire piece (see page 9). Open it up and shred one side until you have a $^1/_8$ inch-band remaining on one edge (see page 8). Cut on the folds, and then cut each piece in half to make 1-inch pieces.

Cut off 10 yards of Brown. Cut it into 1-inch pieces. Trim one end with the mini scallop-edge scissors. Use the remaining Brown as needed.

Cut the 10 yards of Orange into 1-inch pieces. Trim one end with the scallop-edge scissors.

Cut the #3 Basil into $1^3/_4$-inch pieces. Trim the ends to a rounded point (like a leaf tip).

Fold the #100 Basil ribbon at 2 inches. Using this as a measure, accordion fold the entire piece. Open it up and fold in half lengthwise. Shred both sides (see page 8). Leave a $^1/_2$-inch band in the center of the ribbon ($^1/_4$ inch

on each side of the fold). Using scissors, cut on the accordion folds. Cut those pieces in half to make 1-inch pieces, then in half again to make $^1/_2$-inch pieces.

Place just the knot in the clothespin. Do not wind the thead around it. Anchor your clothespin to the table clamp. You will sew this lei with a long thread.

Lay out 4 pieces of Brown, 4 pieces of Orange, and 1 Brown fringe.

❶ Place 1 Orange piece over the Brown piece with the scalloped end extending $^1/_4$ inch. Roll the 2 pieces together into thirds.

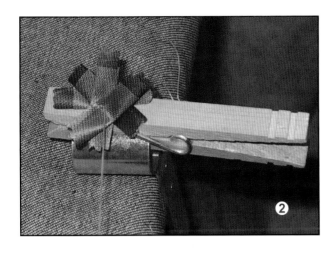

② Without creasing it, hold the flower in the center and sew through the middle. Be sure to have all the flowers facing to the right. Press the 4 down.

③ Sew a small running stitch down the band of the Brown fringe, twisting it on the needle (see photo, page 18). Press it down. This makes 1 set.

Make about 15 sets. Leave the sets loose on the thread until you are ready to arrange them.

To arrange the flowers, fan the first set out to the right. Place the flowers of the second set in between the spaces of the first set, working in a clockwise direction. This is the beginning of the spiral pattern. (See Twisted Dahlia, page 41, step 4.)

After pressing the fringe down, continue setting the flowers in between the previous ones, still working clockwise. Press each flower

down tightly so it will not move. This completes the cigar flower portion. Attach a clothespin to hold your work in place.

Place 1 Basil fringe, 12 Basil pieces, 1 kukui nut, 12 Basil pieces, 1 kukui nut, 12 Basil pieces, and 1 Basil fringe on the table. Sew a small running stitch down the center of the fringe. Pinch (see page 10) each piece of Basil in the center, sew through the sides, and then sew through the first kukui nut. Pinch and sew the next set of Basil, and then sew another fringe. Sew through the next kukui nut. Repeat with another Basil set. Finish with the final fringe. This completes the leaf-and-kukui portion.

The flower and the leaf-and-nut portions together make one complete pattern segment. It takes about 9 of these to finish this lei.

Note: The cigar flowers will move around if they are spaced too loosely. Don't worry if the Brown fringe doesn't open fully; it just shouldn't clump.

Twisted Dahlia

designed by Aunty Lucy

- 80 yards of C&G #9 ($1^1/_4$-inch) Grape ribbon
- 80 yards of C&G #9 ($1^1/_4$-inch) Orchid ribbon
- #6 embroidery needle
- nylon beading thread
- 3 wooden clothespins
- 2 table clamps
- Fiskars Personal Paper Trimmer

Cut Pieces

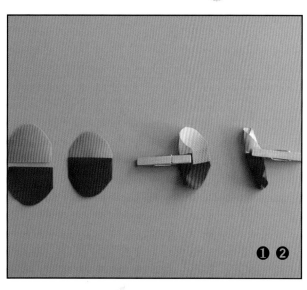

❶ ❷

❸

❶ Cut the Grape and Orchid ribbons into 1 $^1/_2$-inch pieces. Trim the sides (not the ends) of each piece into a dome shape. Leave about $^1/_2$ inch of flat, uncut surface on the ends.

Attach the end of the thread to your clothespin (without wrapping it around the pin) and anchor it to the table clamp. Set 4 pieces of each color in front of you.

❷ Place 1 Grape piece over an Orchid piece with $^1/_4$ inch overlapping. Roll (see Rolling, page 11).

❸ Sew through the middle of the petal, making sure to sew through all the layers. Do not pinch the ends of the ribbon; the petal should be round.

Do the same with the remaining sets of 3 pairs of ribbons. Press all the petals down with the Grape ends to the right.

Sew about 2 feet of petals the same way. Push them down, but not tightly.

Attach the second table clamp with another clothespin about 2 feet from the end of the work with the remaining thread wound around the clothespin. Be sure the thread is taut. This will free your hands to work on the next step.

Now you will arrange the petals. Note: all the instructions from here on will focus on the tips of the Grape ribbon only.

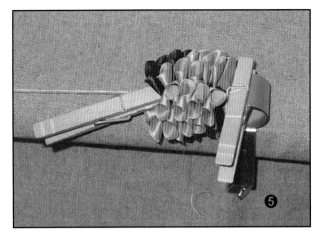

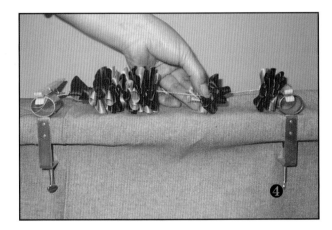

❹ Working in sets of 4, fan the tips of the first set out to the right. Moving over into the first space, place the tips of the second set in between the spaces of the first, working in a clockwise direction. This is the beginning of the spiral pattern. Continue placing each set of petals clockwise in between the petals of the previous set by moving over one space from the first petal of the previous set. Be sure to press each petal down tightly so it will not move.

❺ When all the petals have been arranged, attach the third clothespin to the thread at the end of the work to hold it in place. At this time you will be able to see the design. Remove the second clamp and move it down another 2 feet.

Working with 2 feet of petals at a time, repeat the above instructions.

The lei's pattern may shift from time to time if the petals are not packed down tightly enough during the arranging process. If this happens, fix the pattern by moving the petals.

This lei is not for beginners.

Maui Sunset

created by Aunty Lucy, revised by Coryn Tanaka

- 20 yards of C&G #3 ($^1/_2$-inch) Valeria ribbon
- 20 yards of C&G #3 ($^1/_2$-inch) Orange ribbon
- 2 yards of C&G #3 ($^1/_2$-inch) Belle ribbon
- 2 yards of C&G #40 ($2^1/_2$-inch) Orange ribbon
- 2 yards of C&G #3 ($^1/_2$-inch) Bermuda Pink ribbon
- 2 yards of C&G #5 ($^7/_8$-inch) Old Gold ribbon
- cotton darner
- #6 embroidery needle
- beading thread
- wooden clothespin
- table clamp
- Fiskars Personal Paper Trimmer

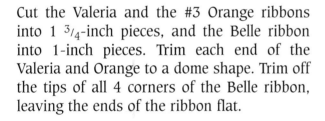

42~

Cut Pieces

Cut the Valeria and the #3 Orange ribbons into 1 $^3/_4$-inch pieces, and the Belle ribbon into 1-inch pieces. Trim each end of the Valeria and Orange to a dome shape. Trim off the tips of all 4 corners of the Belle ribbon, leaving the ends of the ribbon flat.

Mark the #40 Orange at 2 inches and fold. Use this as a measure to accordion fold down the length of the ribbon (see page 9). Unfold and refold the ribbon in half lengthwise. Shred the sides of the ribbon (see page 8) until you have a 1-inch band remaining in the center of the ribbon ($^1/_2$ inch on each side of the fold). With the ribbon folded lengthwise, cut it with scissors from the folded side at the accordion folds, then cut in half to make 1-inch pieces.

Mark the Old Gold ribbon at 2 inches and fold. Use this as a measure to accordion fold down the length of the ribbon. Unfold. Shred from one side until you have a $^1/_8$-inch band

remaining (see page 8). Cut on the folds. Cut the pieces in half to make 1-inch pieces. Repeat with the Bermuda Pink ribbon.

Set out 4 pieces of Valeria, 4 pieces of Orange, 2 pieces of Belle, 1 #40 Orange fringe, 1 Old Gold piece, and 1 Bermuda Pink piece. Pinch and sew through the center of each piece of Valeria (see page 10). Do the same with the Orange and Belle. Sew a small running stitch down the middle of the Orange ribbon. Twist the ribbon around the needle (see photo page 18) and push it down. Pinch and sew the remaining Old Gold and Bermuda Pink pieces. This completes one flower.

Keep repeating the steps in the last paragraph until the lei is done.

1 in.

5/8 in.

3 in.

1 3/4 in.

1 1/4 in.

2 in.

~43

Marking Grid

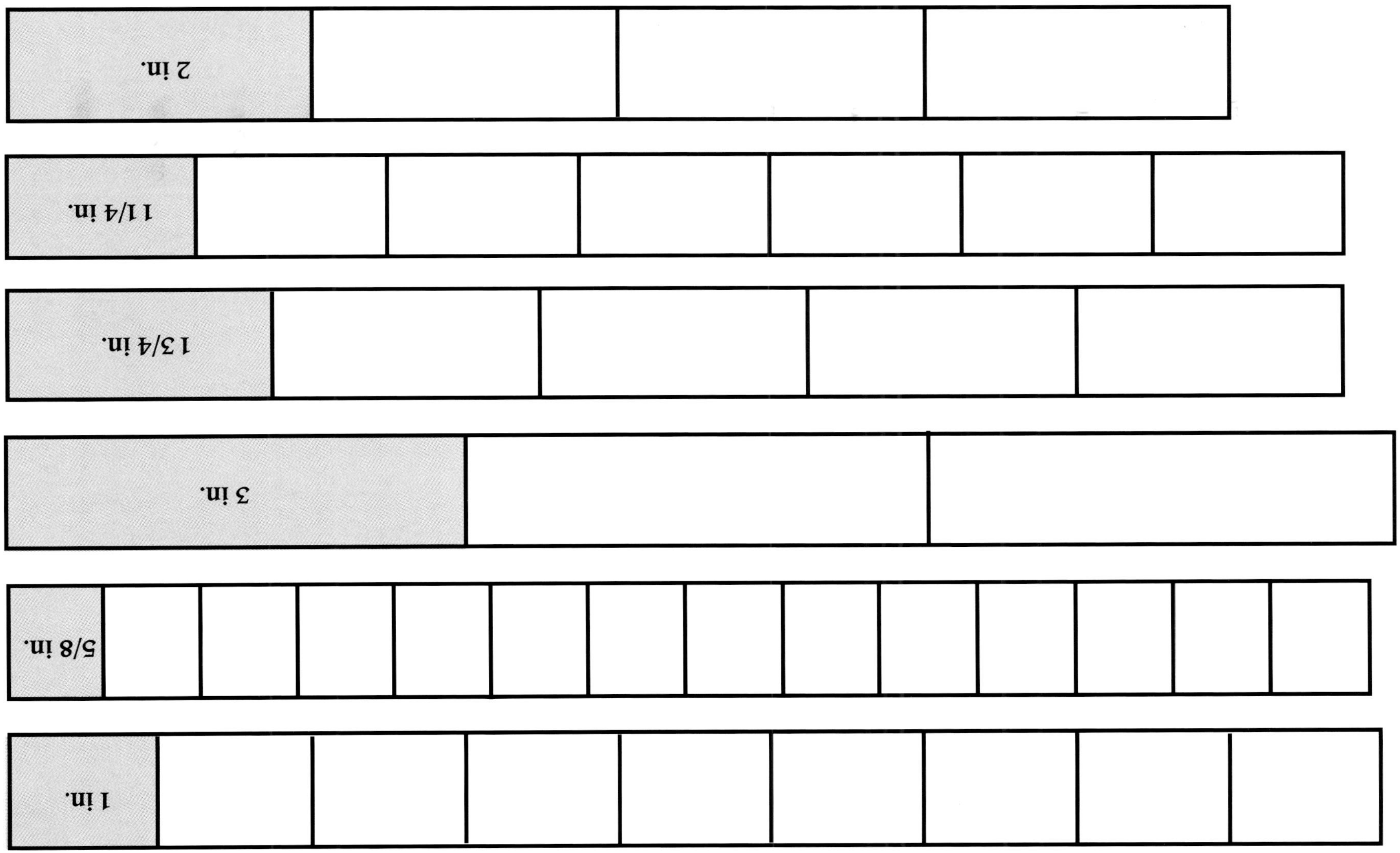

Marking Grid

44~

1/2 in.

2 1/2 in.

5/16 in.

1 1/2 in.

1/4 in.